How

To Become

A

Top

Social

Influencer

Shark Bite Coaching

ISBN: 0615856381
ISBN-13: 978-0615856384

DEDICATION

This book is dedicated to entrepreneurs and business professionals who are ready to take their businesses to the next level.

I wish you luck in your success and hope that I can help even just a little bit.

CONTENTS

THE INTERNET AND INTERACTION

The 21st century is all about innovation and the Internet itself is proof enough. With it, boundaries have been taken down and bonds have been built. The Internet has brought numerous benefits but one that may not have been predicted was its use as a tool for direct interaction, both synchronous and asynchronous.

Since humans are curious creatures, it is easy to understand how man came to utilize the Internet to satisfy a curiosity. If at first, the World Wide Web served the purpose of virtual library, today, it has been transformed into a two-way form of communication (Web 2.0). This type of interaction is much more compelling than simply reading through texts, watching videos, or listening to an mp3 or podcast.

Through this platform built for two-way interaction, people became more engaged, if not more entwined—exchanging ideas with each other via the various social media platforms. Social media did not rise alongside the spread of the World Wide Web. Instead, it took quite a bit longer for the concept of social networking to be developed and for people to take notice. And yet, being viral as it is, 'social media' is almost synonymous with "Internet" nowadays.

If you are wondering how this happened, the answer will take us back to the basic reason people became interested in the Internet in the first place—connectivity.

The concept of social media is very basic—the conversion of daily interactions into a virtual reality space. It transforms an intangible platform into a foundation that can actually launch something. Sounds unrealistic, right?

Simply said, it is not very complicated, it is available and it is current. Social media is a world of its own; it has redefined the meaning and experience of interaction and reality.

Come to think of it, such concepts were simply depicted in futuristic Hollywood movies before and yet, how easily that concept became reality. Social media presented a means of connectivity in a realm that had only been thought of as fantasy; and it not only became reality but an actual "real-time" version of it.

WHY IS SOCIAL MEDIA SO POWERFUL?

Social media is an established realm with participants numbering in the millions because it is information rich. Because of the immediacy and flow of communication, the information is easy to use, free to use and can be manipulated into however an individual wants to use it.

That is why there is no single concept as to why or how social media became powerful. In reality, it is a mix of different aspects/characteristics that catapulted the appreciation and utilization of social media and networking in everyday life and business:

Availability

If there is one good reason why social media is powerful, that is because the platforms are readily and widely available. Out of the seven billion people on earth, more than two billion have direct access to the Internet. These two billion are likewise able to access social media, thanks to the benefit of internet connectivity. Being a social and communication tool, people consider the different social media platforms as their best and fastest means of making an impression. It is where they communicate, socialize, influence, and obtain information.

Because social media is easily accessible, people use it as often as they want to, and there are basically no restrictions.

Equal Playing Field

As for a newbie or starter in social media, Facebook, Twitter, and LinkedIn are the best tools to start with and by adding other popular platforms—make a lasting mark on the web. They don't have to worry about getting left behind because what social media creates is an equal playing field. So basically everyone has the right and opportunity to begin establishing influence, branding, or niching for different purposes, be it business and marketing or simply for the hope of being someone significant online like a top social influencer.

Variety

Social media is powerful because it features variety, which means it is capable of providing a lot of things for people to embrace. For one, it is habit-forming. The majority of Facebook users log in to their accounts at least once every day, and that is because they usually find an interesting post or message (or hope to). Each day presents and offers a new wave of trends, information, and topics to talk about.

Likewise, the kind of content social media users get from the different platforms are so varied that they don't offer any bias, restriction, or segregation. The substance does not center on one topic alone but is available on all levels as well. Availability and content are the two strongest points, which propelled social media into mainstream. But these are not the only reasons why it has become influential, though.

Here are a few less influential, yet still important, reasons behind the absolute acceptance of social media:

Presence

Social media has become incredibly powerful largely because it is the most comprehensive means of establishing an online presence. Whether the presence is intended for business or personal reasons, the notion of being involved in a community has fascinated not just the younger generation, but also the more mature ones.

The possibilities, for one, are endless for online businesses. Social media not only helps them promote businesses regardless of niche, but also provides a platform for maintaining an active online presence, where the greatest number of prospective shoppers and consumers are gathered. Presence is precipitated by web traffic. Social media services and social networking sites generate volumes of web traffic and that corresponds to becoming known and recognized.

Social networking used to be designed for creating personal accounts online and corresponding with friends and family. The concept alone is not just popular because people know about it but because the majority of the Internet population is signing up and getting involved for different reasons. Presence means online visibility. Being visible means having access to information via the fastest means possible and becoming effectively proactive.

Relationships

Building a relationship online begins the moment a person creates an account on any of the social media platforms. Obviously, anyone with a network of friends, relatives, family, and coworkers may also have their own accounts to build his/her virtual network of the same types. The friends and acquaintances of one person are then introduced to others and more relationships are built and nurtured.

But one distinctive aspect of building relationships through social media is that there are basically no ethical or moral standards. Some may be based on personal connection like being a member of a family while others are detached and sometimes even based on lies using pseudonyms, aliases, and false personas. These sorts of intertwined relationships and correspondence can only be found in the world of social media.

For businesses, basically all social media platforms are best utilized for building relationships with both existing and potential clients and customers. Platforms including, but not limited to, Facebook and Twitter, blogs, review sites, and forums offer a huge arena of people converging to discuss similar interests, mostly about things they want to purchase or may be interested in purchasing online. While businesses seem to build genuine relationships with these people, the true purpose is to convince them to either purchase products or avail them of the variety of products and services offered.

For friends and family, the premise is that social media impacts real relationships between real persons. Millions of people have met and eventually gotten together (in various ways) by communicating through the different social media platforms.

Likewise, it is also the most extensive community of people who share the same interests and hobbies. For instance, dog lovers from around the world even have created their own social networking sites where they gather and share information and experiences. Ever heard of MyDogSpace, MyCatSpace, and PetBrags? They sound funny but they do exist.

Conversations

Ideally, the conversational aspect of social media is what humanizes it. For a lot of people, creating an account in Facebook, MySpace, or any other social networking site doesn't always mean they have to use their real identities. But the moment they begin to converse with their "virtual" friends, they begin to reveal their true identities. Real time conversations are a benefit of social media that can never be taken away from any user.

Because of the millions of people signing up, social media is becoming bigger than the Internet itself, in a way that there are countless individuals conversing and chatting every minute.

On LinkedIn, for instance, any member can create a group for free. LinkedIn groups are established for people who share the same interests (in this case, professional networking and development). Interests vary a lot—from sharing content or information, asking questions and providing answers, making business contacts, or simply hoping to meet other people and converse. As soon as the group is created, every member gets the chance to participate in the discussion. There are member-only groups and open groups, to which the difference is obvious. In Facebook, on the other hand, a group chat is possible when you create that group. You add the people you want to invite to join the group conversation while creating the group.

It's Free

But if there is one underlying reason why social media has become so powerful, it's the fact that the majority of the platforms are free to join and participate. The convenience brought by the Internet the first time it was introduced decades ago is reflected in the same way as that of the social media capability today. The impact is plain and simple—revolutionary.

If there was ever a question why social networking sites became rapidly popular in such a short span of time, it is mainly because sign up and registration are free, and they don't intend to charge anything thereafter for the basic use of socializing (the monetization of these sites comes in the form of social gaming, events, premiere memberships, etc).

Social media, particularly social networking sites, are free since they are primarily built as a community rather than a promotional venue. Hence, they are intended to lure as many users as possible in order to expand the platform. Here are a few more specifics:

Facebook—The term comes from an informal name of a book that was given to students at the beginning of the school year at several universities in the United States, the purpose of which is to aid the new students in recognizing other students. Today, Facebook has become the largest online social networking service. With over one billion active users as of 2012, there is some question as to how a social media platform can grow so fast. The best answer is because it is free. The popularity of the site is also attributed to the concept of creating user profiles. By creating an account and profile, the user gets the full luxury and privilege of uploading and posting photos, listing personal interests and activities, contact information, and even personal details. As soon as the account is created, users can communicate with friends who have established their own accounts as well. Regardless of whether the communication is private or public, everything is basically free. Now do you remember those times when you had to pay for every phone call you made, or perhaps for every telegram or fax you sent?

Twitter—Another free online social networking service that rapidly grew in popularity is Twitter. But this time, it is more of a hybrid or combination of social networking and micro blogging—both are still considered to be distinct platforms or types of social media. This free service is unique in a way that it requires its users to post and read text-based messages or posts referred to as "tweets." The site is popular because in a way, it has replaced the mainstream line of communication through paid SMS. What it does is provide a free SMS service or tweets on demand via the Internet to its registered users while the unregistered ones still have the opportunity to read certain tweets. It has even become a very suitable arena for reaching out to famous people and grabbing their interest, through the concept of "followers." As of the publication of this book, Twitter has over 500 million users.

LinkedIn—The concept of free social media is still applicable in LinkedIn, arguably the third most popular in the social networking platform race. But what separates LinkedIn from Twitter and Facebook is that there is a distinct segregation towards professional connections and networking. Hence, it is popularly referred to as a professional networking site. The site allows everyone to register for free. The interface revolves around the concept of "connections." A registered user maintains a collection of people that they have a certain

9

degree of a relationship, and these people are the connections, a term that is quite similar to "friends" in Facebook. But unlike Twitter or Facebook, LinkedIn does not condone or promote flooding and spamming of untargeted messages. Users may be able to invite people to become a connection but the invitee can label or mark the user as a spammer, putting a red flag on that user's account. When the user gets a lot of negative responses or too many red flags, there is a greater likelihood of being banned and the account closed.

Why Is It Free?

It is no secret that the Internet has become a virtual breeding ground for communications for all businesses. Therefore, it is fair to build an impression that every website is established in order to gain something in return, in most cases that would be profits. But why are all major social networking sites free?

The basic and fundamental reason behind the idea of making the registration and membership free is to be able to successfully build a social graph for every interested user. It means that Facebook and others would want to have as many users as possible and build on the resulting connections. In return, they expect that their website will become more like a large marketplace or economy where businesses will begin monetizing them. If social networking sites begin charging for basic accounts, then it is to be expected that many will not be interested in signing up and some existing users may delete or close-out their accounts.

Klout.com

Klout.com is a new and innovative way of viewing social media and social media influence. In fact, a Klout score is entirely based on how influential you are in the entirety of your social media presence. Entirety means the website is linked and works with the likes of the biggest and most popular social networking sites like Facebook, Twitter, and others.

Unlike the mainstream social media platforms, Klout is different because it is not just about communication and correspondence. It is more about bragging rights—at least in the perspective of being a social influencer.

Klout is all about building influence. If the average social media enthusiast creates an account or profile to satisfy this need to correspond and be with other people, signing up on Klout is more about satisfying the need of gauging and monitoring the social influence of that same individual.

The website makes use of data from the user's accounts on various social networking sites including Facebook, Twitter, Google+, and LinkedIn and then builds a profile using the data from these social networking sites. The Klout user profile is then assigned a unique Klout score based on the level of social influence built over time. Hence, the higher the Klout score is, the more extensive the social influence is. Influence, in turn, is measured— say in Twitter—by the number of followers, tweet count, re-tweets, list memberships, etc.

In order to become a true top social influencer, there are some tasks to complete and facts to keep in mind…Read on…

THE SEVEN SITES YOU MUST BE ON

One of the most famous forms of social media is the networking. The realization of a virtual relationship can only be established if one creates an account on one or all of the social networking sites. And the connectivity also depends on which social networking site or sites you create a presence on.

1. Facebook

Undeniably, Facebook is the most popular social networking site. With the number of users topping the one billion mark, it is ubiquitous. Every individual who has created a profile with the site can be connected with any and all of the other users, and this idea alone is the primary reason why social networking is attractive.

Imagine being connected with the rest of the world, despite differences in culture, geography and even personality. Facebook or what is simply referred to as **FB**, is the foremost social networking site to be present on.

A clear advantage of the site from others is its ability to adapt to changes. Though, it may not actually be the first in the field, it is the first to be considered a ground breaker. It has survived various attacks and criticisms and continues to survive them (and even thrive) through constantly upgrading the platform and functionality. It is highly adaptable and yes, trendy.

During the first few years of the site, Facebook's design was almost bare but it worked. And as its popularity increased, so did the number of ways to build a profile, links to connect to, and a stable presence on the web. Besides, no person wants to create an account with a site that is losing ground in the areas of usage and usability, how could you be socially connected (or help your users remain socially connected) if your platform can't keep up, right?

Facebook knows how to dance to the music of current trends and actually, very often dictates the trends. If all you want or wanted was to be present on the Internet, then Facebook is the way to go.

It can fulfill the most basic of all human needs: contact, or in today's terms—working connectivity. Isn't this the down and dirty purpose of social media? Though developed prematurely for the benefit of Harvard students, the developers thought it would be best if the site was launched to the general public and not limited only to Ivy leaguers. The site places a high value on connectivity without any regard for professional status, demographic profile or any other reason beyond just wanting to connect with "friends."

Facebook allows you to amass a number of friends, mostly giving you the chance to reconnect with former classmates or even loved ones. This is actually the foremost reason why Facebook became so incredibly successful; all the other applications that one can enjoy with the site came years later.

What You Don't Know About Facebook: For some, Facebook is simply about signing up as a member and then getting a profile page based on your own customization. But what really makes it very interesting is that you can catch up with anyone at almost an instant, even if that someone is from your distant past. Have you ever wondered where your first grade best friend is now or what he's up to? Do you want to see your childhood crush and what she looks like at age 30? While these questions were left hanging a while back, it has become a lot more convenient these days to answer these queries simply by typing names into the site's search box. Do you think they're NOT part of the one billion users of this social networking site?

But there are things that most people didn't know Facebook could do, and being aware of them will give you an edge in your race to becoming a top social influencer. For instance, there is actually a way to track and monitor your own page's success. This feature is handy for those creating accounts for business purposes. By clicking the "View Insights" button in the upper right corner, Facebook will display charts containing information about the account activities and success such as user information and page interactions. Aside from the likes and comments all users know about, a graph will display the number of page views, user feedback, and even a comprehensive look at which web domains are contributing to the traffic of your account's pages. The data can be exported to a Microsoft Excel spreadsheet for filing or further analysis.

Another important component of Facebook that few users know about is the document collaboration feature. The feature is a great way to expand a user's influence. In the group page, there's a tab called "Docs" located at the top. Once the button called "create a doc" is clicked, a text-only document will be created and everyone in that group has the ability to edit the document, hence, the term collaboration. Whenever the document is freshly edited and saved, a status update is given to the other group members.

And although the social networking site is built for people to interact, there is no guarantee that everyone does this particularly well. In fact, the average number of friends a user had as of the end of 2012 was 150. But in this number, the average user will only interact and communicate regularly with seven of them.

Overall though, with a few hits and misses, Facebook continues to fuel the human desire to stay connected. It remains the social networking authority and ensures a strong online presence for you.

2.　Twitter

The idea of building Twitter came out of nowhere. It was actually designed to be what it is really today—by writing or posting something that you don't think about. It's a spur of the moment and whatever comes to mind, you just speak it out (or tweet it out as the case may be).

This is a social networking site that has become successful in little ways. Unlike Facebook, Twitter did not become an instant success. It had battled with usability issues. There was once a time when Facebook was ALL that social networking needed and Twitter was one of the others that were deemed nearly "unnecessary."

Yet Twitter quieted doubts with adaptability and a unique concept of "being known". Twitter invented the idea of a 140-character message or tweet. Because the idea of merely being present on the web was quickly becoming stale, Twitter reinvented the lure of wanting to be present by truly being present to the level of individual thoughts and ideas.

In a society where "appearance" matters greatly, the right word play within these 140-characters can garner a second look at the very least, or a follower if you prove to impress. Tweets and followers are the great concepts of Twitter.com. The users of this micro-blogging site enjoy real-time updates that come in quick thoughts and notes as opposed to reading a "novel".

Famous personalities often interact with their admirers and fans on the site as well, it is one of the most preferred sites to interact with a celebrities' fan base. Also, trending topics is one of the quirky ideas of the site, with it; users of the site can chime in and/or participate in the "trending" event. Such events are known to cause a stir if not a raucous for various political and socially relevant issues. With only 140 characters (or less if you want others to be able to retweet your tweet), it is a guaranteed way to develop the concise writer in every account owner.

In comparison to other social networking sites, Twitter.com is probably the first website to have established a secure on-the-go version. Through evolving technology, tweeting became much more convenient and farther reaching with the launch of the mobile version.

More so, the idea of tweeting really caught on because people do not need their screens flooded with status updates. With Twitter, individuals acquire a following because of their creativity and ability to grab attention with short messages, comments, quips, quotes, etc.

These are just some of the reasons why "twitterverse" is continuously gaining ground as a force to reckon with in the social networking arena. It works as a social connection for both personal and business purposes so unlike the more famous Facebook, one can actually maintain a more professional tone with Twitter.

But just like Facebook, it is a social networking site with several secrets, and they are actually pretty interesting.

What You Don't Know About Twitter: Haven't you asked about the name or personality of the Twitter bird? Yes, that bird has an official name and it's Larry! And in case you don't know why it's Larry; the bird is named after a Boston Celtics great, Larry Bird.

And finally, not a lot of people, especially those who have Twitter accounts know that the social networking website itself didn't really invent or conceptualized some of its most popular features including retweets, hash tags, replies, and social ads. Each one of them was created by either users or developers engaged in the development of the platform. They were truly inventions based on a pressing need or inclination to do things better.

3. Google+

Google may have been a pioneer in the freedom of exchanging and sharing information online without limits, but it is way behind in the development of its own social media platform, called Google+.

As a social networking site, Google+ entered the game very late. Though Google may have created the idea of 'googling', it was slower on the uptake as a social networking site. The developers of the premium search engine grabbed the opportunity of creating a profile, linking and connections just after social networking emerged as a winning concept. Though, even late in the game, Google+ is quickly becoming a formidable opponent.

The plus (+) in creating a profile with the site is the segregation of identities. Facebook may have answered all the social needs over the Internet, but it has also overcrowded it as well. Being friends with your grade school classmate or reconnecting with a long lost neighbor may have a warm effect but getting minute by minute updates from your boss or wife may not be as alluring as getting one from an interesting friend.

Google+ was developed for the sole purpose of helping individuals remain socially connected with a more appropriate tone dependent upon the circle you are communicating with. One size really doesn't fit all. It actually helps individuals create a more professional outlook thus, it is a safer social network for people who would rather be known for their great projects rather than what they do on their weekends.

Any person who creates an account with Google+ can also set up links with other applications but unlike Facebook, Google+ accounts are not meant to simply make friends or reignite lost flames, it is a site worth investing time in because it is good for business.

What You Don't Know About Google+: Yes, you have heard it here FIRST—Google+ isn't actually a social networking site. An understandable mistake as the user interface has many similarities to Facebook and Twitter. However, it is built as a social media platform intended to boost presence and integrity in the world's biggest search engine—Google. The "1+ Button" found in Google+ is intended to feed Google, the search engine. What it does to the account is build and match more targeted ads, which in turn leads to more profits for business-oriented accounts.

And because more data is good for any business, at least in the Google+ perspective, one advantage of the website when it comes to influencing social media is that the user is actually given a chance to post, not just a tweet or send a status update, but an entire blog or article. As a result, the more content is fed to Google, the more likely it is to increase online visibility and the faster you can become an extremely effective social influencer.

4.   YouTube

Without a doubt, YouTube.com is a hit. As successful as any other social networking site can be, YouTube has commanded the market in a different and yet highly utilizable approach. It is visually appealing and very satisfying for both its registered users and those who just browse the site.

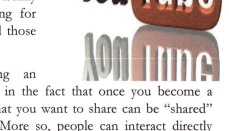

The allure of creating an account with YouTube lies in the fact that once you become a registered user, any video that you want to share can be "shared" through the website itself. More so, people can interact directly with others who also viewed a particular video through the video's designated comments pane.

And because YouTube understands the concept of entertaining people more than any other, the website allows people not only to watch videos but also to share their own videos as well. It is a rich source of raw materials that are enjoyed by watching—not reading.

It is important to create an account on this site because you will create a reliable history and you can upload any video you like…Fun! Fun! Millions of account holders provide enough reasons for logging into your account. The 'You' in the YouTube definitely means personalized entries as there are looser restrictions in uploading personal videos than most other sites impose. As a matter of fact, there is little to no censorship or filtering in YouTube and practically everyone can access and see the videos. For some, it may be quite dangerous for young ones to view gross and violent videos, but the concept this platform really isn't and never was intended for young kids.

In the lines of social networking, Youtube.com sparks the entertaining side of every individual and that is why it remains one of the most visited sites for any purpose.

Purpose wise, there seems to be a lot of reasons why people visit YouTube or create their own accounts.

Educational: The library has become nearly obsolete due to the fact that the web provides a million folds of information compared to even the biggest library in the world. But information these days isn't limited to text and images anymore. The latest trend is motion picture or video, and arguably YouTube is the biggest contributor of video knowledge and information on the web.

YouTube can be utilized as a rich source of information that includes video tutorials, seminars, webinars, how-to, instructional, documentaries, critiques, and a lot more. For instance, some of the best professors and instructors around the world have even recorded video tutorials and lectures made available for public viewing. However, not everything is free because some others will require you to subscribe in order to access the lectures. Unlike before where you became worried if you missed a class, now you can totally make up for it by having your own 'personal' video lecture via YouTube.

Entertainment: But the educational purpose of YouTube is perhaps only a pint of what the site is all about. For the average user, the main purpose of visiting the site on a day-to-day basis is to look for fun in the form of video entertainment. These people are the ones responsible for sharing, downloading, and uploading the videos for the sake of entertaining other people. Arguably the most viewed clips are those that contain funny humor and comedy-inspired activities. Apart from that, entertainment also includes music videos, sports highlights, full-length movies, trailers, documentaries, TV shows, and a lot more. So if you happen to visit YouTube for the first time, it is probably because you're looking for some entertainment or a bit of humor.

Instructional Videos and How-To's: Google is the most popular search engine, but YouTube is making its case. But instead of all kinds of search results, the site only provides videos—and since Google now owns YouTube, there is no longer a competition. The main purpose of using YouTube as a search engine is to look for instructional videos, how-to videos, etc. As a result, it has become relatively easy these days to engage in do-it-yourself projects at home with the assistance of these instructional videos. Information can also be in the form of fixing things like a computer, car, gadgets, or practically everything that needs fixing. If you don't believe it, just type in whatever you want to fix in the YouTube search box and you'll see what I mean.

Sports Reviews and Highlights: Sports enthusiasts and avid fans use YouTube to review or relive memorable moments of their favorite teams. The majority of sports channels use the YouTube platform to upload game highlights, previous sports spectacles and events like the Super Bowl, NBA Finals, World Cup, or Wimbledon. Fans and viewers can find games they missed and watch them for free. And because YouTube has the largest and most extensive database there is, practically every sporting event is covered.

Professional and Business Purposes: Finally, YouTube is not just for the mainstream, average, or traditional user. Interest can extend deep into professional purposes. What this means is that even professionals will visit the site for purposes that are in one way or another related to their profession or building his/her business. In fact, most businesses today are establishing an online presence and uploading their own videos and commercials for the purpose of marketing and advertising whatever it is they are selling.

From the business perspective, videos that appear to be informational are actually a way to lure potential customers who might be interested in the products or services they offer. The main purpose of the business-oriented video is to direct interested parties (potential customers) to the user's official business website.

5.   Hi5

Some might be surprised that Hi5 is listed here. But no one can deny that it has actually been consistently growing and expanding since 2008. Although Facebook, YouTube, Twitter, and even LinkedIn may have overtaken Hi5, it is still very relevant. It can be described more as the popular social networking site you've never heard of. Although the site reached about 10 million members as early as 2005, its success has never been documented because it focused its growth on the international stage [like launching a Spanish version of the social networking site quickly followed by other languages]. It is actually one of the most popular social networking sites in the Latin American region. But interaction wise, there's really nothing special since it's more like the typical site wherein everyone can register and become a member, create a personal profile, share photos and info, post messages, and play online games.

6. Pinterest

Pinterest is not a new concept in the world of social networking sites but unlike sharing loads of information in the form of text and characters, Pinterest users rely on images to create their connections. The concept is more like a YouTube only that photographs are pinned and/or re-pinned, instead of videos.

The beauty of Pinterest is that people can develop relationships based on captured images rather than having a common alma mater or home town or unique status updates. If an individual pins a picture which is subsequently liked by another, then a connection is automatically established.

Pinterest.com "pinpoints" what someone actually enjoys more than any other site and then gives full access to other images falling into the same category as the image you liked.

More than answering the need to be socially relevant, Pinterest is becoming relevant in the marketing realm as well. It is becoming a reliable source of links that can actually create a consumer base for different brands. It offers an attractive front page, engaging enough for an individual to click on links that will actually convert into sales.

Any individual who wants to learn about a business, a product or any topic of general interest can easily find unique sites that teach, share, and allow others to share it too. In comparison with other image uploading social pages, Pinterest operates on a formula that is easier to handle, more visually enticing and was launched at a time when interest in the way other social networking websites functioned had started to decline.

7. LinkedIn

A LinkedIn member gets to develop a profile in a social context that is more professionals than the other platforms mentioned already. It sets the tone for connectivity in a manner that can make connections based on a less personal connection.

It has appropriate settings, which one can choose from in order to secure information and predetermine what information will be accessible to others—connections or otherwise. Entrepreneurs like to launch their products through this site because it has been programmed to allow for easy marketability.

Though signing up is free, upgrading to a paid account has proven to be a winning move on LinkedIn. Not only can you develop a better interaction with your market, but you can also keep consumers and potential clients informed in a unique manner that works best for businesses.

LinkedIn remains one of the best social networking magnets because it has been developed precisely under the assumption that social connection is necessary in creating better marketing partners and professional relationships. LinkedIn believes that this can be done in a manner that need not divulge unnecessary personal information but just enough to make an impression and a deeper professional connection.

CREATE A MAGNETIC PROFILE

Social networking became an instant hit because it is a creative method with various options of platforms for unique types of interaction. For a long time, people used the Internet to retrieve ideas and relay information—there was little time left for relationship building. The process was purely a one-way interaction and people quickly lost interest. Thanks to the 21st century, social media and various other types of technologies integrated the need to interact with each other.

And yet, it does not all begin and end with the creation of a profile or page. Whether one has decided to start a profile with the most marketable social networking platform or not, the opportunity to build relationships is not an immediate privilege. Like any other relationships, social networks have to be nurtured too.

Just like with the normal daily and physical interaction, people need to spend time building a better rapport via their profiles on the Internet in order to remain interesting. Most specifically, there are certain activities you must engage in to become a top social influencer.

1. Be Virtually Present

All kinds of relationships need certain reassurances that a bond or connection actually exists. Though there is no physical relationship, social networks require their users to constantly update their profiles and statuses to maintain a list of followers, fans, friends, and connections. This is the basic ingredient in creating not just a list of followers but virtual friends as well.

It is not enough that you have a Facebook account or a mobile Twitter account. You have to do more than that—tap into interests, choose unique links to share, and post an update at least once a day. Friend requests must be answered as soon as possible in order to avoid relaying the feeling that you are not open to the idea of being friends. Virtual rejection is just as hurtful as face-to-face rejection.

Being virtually present is really all about making your presence felt in a consistent manner. In most instances, those who have social networking accounts will log in occasionally and provide updates from time to time. But the hope of being a top social influencer means more than just updating your status. It means you need to aim at being present and up-to-date with all newsworthy items or current events relevant to your interests. In simple terms—you have to be there.

2. Be Interactive

The promise of social media is the enhanced idea of communication: two-way interaction. Therefore, in order for people to follow you on your social page, you must be ready to interact. You must not merely watch as your friends' lists build up but make an effort to react to your own pages' activities.

After a friend request, take the time to be the first one to say hi, or better yet, 'like' their posts too. By being responsive, others will feel a warm and open reception and will nurture the feeling for a long time; it could even lead to a follower, recommendation, or endorsement.

If you are on the social network to build relationships, being reactive to other people's activity will earn you respect just for noticing. If you are on it for marketing, the same concept applies only if it will earn you more money. Therefore, to be on different social networks for different reasons will require a greater attention to detail.

And yes, detail and interest are the two most important facets of being interactive. Social media is based on a two-way interaction process wherein people communicate and correspond for several different purposes. But if you are aiming at becoming someone relevant and influential in social media, you have to understand the need to reply to messages, projecting a high level of interest for people and virtual friends from all walks of life, and making them feel like you're interested in them.

3. Be Profile Savvy

Do not leave your profile to chance and never assume that because you've got your profile up that others will immediately want to connect with you. People can reject requests too, you know, so you better be ready to sell yourself virtually. Your profile need not always show your face, it can always reflect your interests too. In fact, it's not just about faces and how beautiful you are in your profile.

Being profile savvy means you put emphasis on the details—the things that you can add on your profile for people to find it interesting and in some ways, intriguing.

Other people use a profile that reflects their choice of music, and this impresses others who like the same genre, and it will prompt them to check out your page once in a while. The important thing is to have something to lure people to your page over and over again with the anticipation of something new each time.

Stay away from scary images or pictures that can be too offensive. Remember, you are on the social network to get attention; not to repel it. Sensitivity is likewise important, be it cultural, generational, racial, or otherwise. If you are hoping to become a wholesome example and a top social influencer, be sure to get positive attention, not negative. With that in mind, we go to the next "do" of building a magnetic profile.

4. Watch Your Content

First of all, what you post is what gets your page attention. Regardless of which social networking site you are on, you must always bear in mind that what you put into it reflects your self-image. Though some might argue this point, the graphics, the updates and whatever content you plaster on your wall really matters to those who would befriend or connect with you.

If you upload images, videos, or words that seem callous, people may see you as a mere tool. If you go in heavy, some may stay away from you because of the drama. You must know how to gauge the situation and study the feedback after you have placed something on your wall.

A little bit of negativity will not hurt but it will not gain you friends or followers either. So that may defeat the very purpose of you creating an online profile, right? Marketers must always be on the safe side and on social networks; people are all seeking the same thing: attention.

Your content will tell a lot about you and surely, it will get you some attention. It just has to be the right kind of attention so that it will benefit you in other ways.

5. Be Real

The Internet is filled with pretentious people and because there is no way for people to actually confirm all your claims, you can say anything you want in order to impress. But in reality, false stories will get you nowhere and will hurt your reputation in the long-run. The truth ALWAYS comes out.

Sometimes, because you are not being true, you will easily slip and reveal your true colors. When this happens, not only will you lose face but because it is a social network, your reputation may be put on the line. News travels fast—especially in cyber space.

Potential friends and customers need to feel that you are sincere and saying some things that are not truly reflective of the real you can end a promising relationship before it has had a chance to bloom.

6. *Learn*

If you want to increase the traffic to your site, you must take a cue from the experts. This is a proven way of enhancing your chances of adding friends, visits, followers and even sales, that is if you're using social media to market for your online business.

Understanding how people get so many friends and followers can be your shortcut and save you time and stress. Social networks are all about getting attention and having others talk about your page, your content, your ideas, etc. There are so many DIY articles posted on the Internet, you should probably read them too. [You can also check out From Small to Social in 30 Days—Business Owners & Managers on Amazon for helpful tips and timelines.]

Keep in mind if it has already worked, it will most likely improve your chances of optimizing your site as well. So why not read some and add not just friends and followers but increase traffic as well, right?

A 'FOLLOWER' WHO 'LIKES' YOU?

The rules of engagement in developing relationships remain the same: whether it's a physical one or a virtual one. Sometimes, affiliations that develop over the web will require more attention than one that is nurtured through daily exposure.

One has to make an effort to be virtually present; this is the first step in drawing attention to your website or profiles. If you analyze the situation, the battle for social networking dominance applies to its users as well. Not that you need to own the top profile or have the most friends, but rather a social page that gets noticed and is visited often.

A social networking account can only be effective if one is able to find old acquaintances and develop new ones. In all honesty, it does not even depend on who you are creating ties with but mostly in new people wanting to build a connection with you.

There are some rules in being an effective social page owner and it is worth understanding why with social networking sites, it is not about the quantity of the updates but rather who watches for your updates. Here are a few bits of advice that may help:

1. Be Attractive

If you want attention then you must invest in your social profile. The great thing about the different forms of social media is that it understands and translates the concept of beauty. Installed within each website or profile is the technology of changing themes.

It is understandable that a recently created profile will still use a default theme but when a person does not even attach his or her own photo, people will quickly lose interest. It often creates the impression that the owner of the account can't or doesn't want to take time to build an attractive page or become known.

There is doubt whether that person can actually be present and interactive and may not be worth building a relationship with. Posting a pretty picture will definitely draw attention to your page. Therefore, the first rule in effectively building relationships via the social networks is to be as attractive as you can be. If you do not have the face for it, then build a site that will take the place of a pretty face.

2. Be Responsive

Whenever your site gets attention—receives a question or gets a re-pin—try to reciprocate the act. Not that you have to follow every other follower but just be attentive with the activities occurring within your account.

If you posted a video on YouTube and an individual commented, as the uploader, you must be ready to provide a reply. Not that it is your responsibility but it reflects that you are present, willing to interact, and there is an actual person behind that effective post.

In all honesty, one of the biggest doubts of social networking is the humanity behind it all. Because it is easy to create a profile, people want to make sure that you are not only interested in amassing a number of followers or friends but that you are actually willing to build and nurture a relationship.

3. Be Respectful

If you get a criticism, accept it. Criticisms are easily given on the different social media platforms. Even if you create an attractive page, you can still get stumped. This is one of the givens of the Internet, the power to say anything that you want to say.

Even under anonymity, you should be ready for whatever responses your page gets you. There are some people who are forced to close their social pages because of bad press or harassment. Sometimes, this is a better move than having to answer back and risk perpetuating the negativity.

You have to remember that your social network is not a way to make enemies but is supposed to be a means to build new relationships. Bad mouthing is never a good way of starting lasting relationships.

4. Be Creative

Boring gets you nowhere with social media pages and profiles, even if you have the most attractive profile picture. If you are not creative, people will start to unfollow you. Instead of simply posting pictures, create a .gif in its place. Not only will it please your followers but it will also keep them visually satisfied.

If you are a blogger, do not just write extensive paragraphs of text. Break long paragraphs into shorter ones—this not only helps people understand your ideas better but the mere sight of one bulky paragraph after another is too heavy and people just won't read it. Shorter lines will be more enticing to read, and this is a tactic that has worked for others, why not let it work for you?

Use images to depict your ideas or themes you are trying to convey. Not only will it break the monotony but can even help the reader imagine your ideas as opposed to just reading them. You have to always take the point-of-view of the person you are trying to attract. If it takes longer than a minute to take it all in, then you need to do something clever to shorten the suspense. You have to remember, the Internet is full of information and people may just be looking for some entertainment.

5. Be Lawful

Not all people who visit your profile page actually like you, or they may claim they do but they do not always have too. One of the easiest ways to gain more hate than love on the Internet is to claim images, ideas, or concepts that are not actually yours.

Blogging sites often allow people to re-blog other files that belong to someone else and it is easy to do so. There is often an 'easy to click' link that is set up to do this which retains the ownership information with the original person who posted it. Incorporate this practice into your processes and not only will people appreciate that you do the right thing, but they may like following you as well.

MAINTAINING YOUR STATUS

Facebook has been rallying with their millions of critics, they have been evading the possibility of losing the top spot as a social network because they are constantly updating, upgrading, and evolving to meet the needs and desires of the market. You must be ready to do this for your site as well—to keep interest from waning.

You do not have to have a team of experts behind you (although it helps...www.social-media-management-group.com), but knowing and implementing the right moves will keep things in perspective.

1. Be Relevant

In order to sustain interest in your profile page, you must post, update regularly or start conversations that are relevant to current issues and trends. If you belong to a Pinterest page that caters to sports, then you must engage in a conversation with someone belonging to the same group about sports. Do not deviate from the central topic as you are still trying to establish a common ground and maintain status.

If you have already progressed from mere members of the site, then maybe that will be the time that you can start talking about other issues and trends. Relevance is important in establishing and maintaining connectivity. You have to keep in mind that people follow your posts and once you begin showing disinterest in what was believed to be your central theme; people will stop tracking your activities and may withdraw from your network.

2. Join A Community or A Group

In order to maintain a position in social networking circles, you must also be willing to join a group or community. You can find a lot of communities online that have the same interests as you. Joining your account with these groups will help keep your account active and attractive to relationship builders. Not only that, you can get more exposure if you seek out the support of other people with similar interests.

Groups can help promote your page: other people who may not know about you will get a chance to glimpse at your social page just from it being mentioned in your group and these are targeted relations and good prospect traffic. Another good thing about community groups on the Internet is that, it increases credibility. When people see that various groups or credible individuals have approved you, they will credit you for it. Thus helping in the growth and maintenance of your social network, which is more important if you want to be truly influential.

3. Create More Than One Account With More Websites

This is important in order to be able to keep up with the trends. Not that you are anticipating closure of one website but creating more than one account has proven to be beneficial because it reflects how socially "present" you can be.

This is important because there are certain applications that work best with specific sites. There is no monopoly of expertise with social networking and so in order to maximize the benefits, one should be ready to associate themselves with a more capable and popular website to promote their site for them.

Take for example image sharing—Pinterest is a great social networking site for it. The site is fast becoming a top influential site when it comes to image sharing and then it is better able to distribute your images on a wider scale. Your picture can be better appreciated if launched from a platform that actually dominates the market.

Facebook is not a great blogging site and so if this is how you want to be present on the web, then you must open an account with a website that caters to bloggers or start your own with a relevant domain name.

4. Be Attentive

Social media works because there is constant interaction so if you are really interested in keeping your friends or followers, you must never allow your social network to lose its spark. You can prevent this from happening by being attentive.

Be ready to post updates regularly about events, trends, news, etc…or simply reply to messages or queries. Do not just keep liking all the posts of your friends.

Sometimes, the wrong reaction can be costly, so just like in real life—know when to react and when not to.

5. Be Ready To Upgrade

There are some social networks that require subscribers/account holders to upgrade to premium accounts in order to maximize some of the better features. Doing so will increase the appeal of and traffic to your website. This is especially true for accounts that are used for business and marketing. So if you have to do this in order to bring in the money, why not?

Social connectivity does not only mean that you own a social networking account, it is even more than having more friends than your best friend. What actually matters is that you are on the Internet, have enough people interested in your ideas and keeping them interested for an extended period of time. If you can manage all three, then you will forever be socially connected, relevant, and extremely influential.

WHAT TOOLS ARE RIGHT FOR YOU?

Very seldom can you find a person who owns only one social media account. This is not a bad thing; in fact it is the trend in order to be able to keep up with the emergence of too many websites all promoting online connectivity.

This is acceptable even within social networks as reflected by the various links present with each website. There are various tools that help individuals manage their multiple accounts and make more profit from them.

The key to your ideal time management is to have the right social media management tool in place and accurately set up to manage your accounts. Failure to keep up with everything else happening in and around your social profile can make or break the quality of your online connectivity. This eliminates the need to sign into each account individually to manage, post, etc…and, of course, it keeps all your accounts in one dashboard so it's much easier for you to see them all as a whole.

But before you choose which tool/platform to manage your multiple accounts, you must have an idea of what your requirements are to make your tasks easier. This is important so that you will actually pick the best account manager for your needs.

And… if you have multiple accounts, you may want to look into private proxies to protect your accounts from potentially getting shut down.

1. Is Your Social Network Supported?

There would be no sense in downloading an application to manage your multiple accounts if your social networks/platforms are not supported. You have to check that it will be able to manage at least four social networking sites [ideally those that you have accounts on]. There would be no point in using one if it can only manage one or two accounts, right? You must plan for more accounts to cover your various markets, products, personalities, etc (if applicable).

2. Is It Readable?

You have to make sure you actually like the format of the user interface that you will be working within and processing updates through for your multiple social networking accounts. Though, there is very little difference among the top sites, the arrangement of the user interface will affect your time investment, learning curve, and level of aggravation in the long run.

3. How Will You Get It?

There are some social media tools that need to be downloaded to run locally on your computer, while some are hosted and run on the web. Because accessibility is key, you should take into consideration this feature before deciding on one.

4. Is It Free?

Not all applications from the Internet come as freebies; this includes social media tools too. Though almost every other application comes for free, you must first understand the limitations of the free versions versus the paid versions. Because honestly sometimes, there are so many roadblocks with a free application that it is even worse than not using one at all.

5. Can It Deliver?

With the increase of social media platforms, comes the rise in the number of online tools to manage them. One of the more important questions to ask before choosing a social media account management tool is to understand just how much it can actually do for you. Without having to worry you, you must choose to associate all your accounts with one management tool that can manage your tasks for you and do so in a secure and efficient manner.

Also, while preparing to write the marketing plan, you will discover that different members of your company will have different ideas about the current situation and the elements therein. You can use this opportunity to compare different aspects of the market against one another.

TOP SOCIAL MEDIA TOOLS

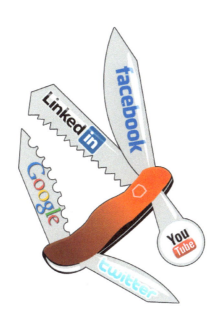

1. HootSuite (www.hootsuite.com)

HootSuite is the top social media management tool that helps optimize multiple social networking accounts. It has a well-integrated system that helps monitor the activity occurring within your site and even with the sites and links that you follow as well.

The advantage of HootSuite compared to other social media management tools is that it supports a wider variety of social networks and keeps adding platforms to its menu of functionalities. It also comes with a free trial before requesting users to pay for a more advanced version via a monthly subscription fee.

And because HootSuite does not need to be downloaded from the Internet, your computer will not be stripped of precious memory or processing speed and it can be accessed from anywhere. There are a lot of advantages that one can enjoy with HootSuite, and it is becoming the top choice for people who want an effective management tool that is easy to use for their social media accounts.

2. TweetDeck (www.tweetdeck.com)

TweetDeck is as famous as HootSuite but it works more effectively for an individual who has a large following in their Twitter accounts. A good thing about TweetDeck is that it is nicely organized and yet remains highly customizable. There are some usable features that come free with every download of Tweetdeck on your desktop.

But on the lowdown because TweetDeck needs to be downloaded from the Internet, it takes up a lot of memory space. Also, it only supports a limited number of social networking accounts. But on the upside, TweetDeck is free to use for as long as you like. There is an app available as well, but true functionality is more likely in the Desktop Version.

3. Buffer (www.bufferapp.com)

Buffer has so many functions similar to HootSuite. It is classified as a smart and convenient means of scheduling content across different social media accounts. It works like a virtual queue wherein one can fill their accounts with content and then set up posting schedules throughout the day or week.

The main advantage of Buffer is that it automates content delivery by way of providing consistent social media scheduling for an entire week. The owner of the social media accounts is relieved of the responsibility of micro-managing the delivery and posting times of the content. Together with an application they call as BufferApp, you can also check out the analytics, specifically about the engagement and status of the posts.

4. SocialOomph (www.socialoomph.com)

SocialOomph is not as popular, but it is one of the easiest to use. It is a neat web tool that offers several productivity and enhancement tools intended for managing social media networks and accounts. There are a lot of things you can do with it for your social networking profiles and accounts including Facebook, Twitter, LinkedIn, Plurk, and even some blogs.

In Twitter alone, the useful features include the ability to schedule tweets, track keywords, view retweets and mentions, inbox cleanup, auto-follow, and more. It is a very productive social media management tool used widely by online businesses.

WHAT ARE YOU WAITING FOR?

Social media and networking is here to stay and more and more people are enjoying the advantages that it brings to their level of social influence. The fun side of social connectivity is that it is becoming less and less complicated to engage in. More fun and less complication—these are the great benefits of social media today, which is attracting more and more people to sign up for at least one social network account.

As developers are quick to improve their social networking sites, users are quick to discern which site they want to associate themselves with. That is why social networking is a very interactive form of media—both inside and out.

The idea of social media is to integrate interaction with technology without discounting the need for human connection. Do you get the drift? This is not difficult to understand either; the most important idea that can be derived from everything we know about social networking is the fact that it can be used to influence people.

Therefore, to be socially relevant nowadays, you must choose to create an account with a social networking site that can actually get you noticed and establish your presence. If you choose to sign up for an account with a website that has not proven to be popular or influential, then you might not get what you think you signed up for.

You must be able to manipulate the Internet to your own needs and not the other way around. The Internet has nearly unlimited doors and windows that one can use in order to grab attention, launch a product and make sales. It's up to you to exploit them.

In all honesty, social connectivity goes beyond the idea of establishing connections nowadays, what works better is if you can actually draw more traffic to your website or blog. By traffic, we mean attention, interaction, lingering connections, and conversions (if applicable).

Everything can come together easily because everything is available on the Internet. All one has to do is make the right choices and use the appropriate platform to launch their online presence. The social media tree has so many branches that it can only be effective if you participate in those that are mainstream before expanding down a branch more specific to your interests, needs, or products.

ABOUT THE AUTHOR

Cassandra Fenyk is a dynamic marketer, speaker, and motivator with extensive experience in various B2B and B2C industries, and unlike many other website and social media consultants, she is also an established marketing professional with nearly 20 years of experience in developing and directing business-to-consumer and business-to-business market penetration strategies. She has spent the majority of her career entrenched in branding, messaging, strategic planning, and project management. She has a keen understanding of the selling process and the critical steps between the initial message, the final sale, and post-sale relationship maintenance. Combined with her knowledge and experience in managing social media and website SEO programs, these traits make her a great source of information and an invaluable resource for your business.

Most recently, Ms. Fenyk started her coaching business focusing on start-ups, small businesses, and entrepreneurs; and all the characteristics that entails. Shark Bite Coaching (www.sharkbitecoaching.com) is that business and if you would like more personalized assistance in avoiding common business pitfalls, overcoming obstacles to your business growth, and getting your business moving in the right direction, ask her and set up an appointment to discuss your ideas and goals.

**LOOK FOR MORE BUSINESS-BUILDING
AND BUSINESS EXCELLENCE BOOKS
BY SHARK BITE COACHING
ON AMAZON**

Shark Bite Coaching
PO Box 373
Florham Park, NJ 07932
shark@sharkbitecoaching.com

A Note to the Reader:

This guide has been written to provide information about becoming a true social networker with the ability to influence others. As with technology, platforms and functionality on the Internet are evolving faster than anyone could imagine. It is nearly impossible to keep up with all the changing details. That being said, every effort has been made to make this guide as complete and accurate as possible. However, there may be mistakes in typography or content. Also, this book provides information only up to the publishing date. Therefore, this guide should be used as such—not as the ultimate source of definitive and final information on social networking.

www.sharkbitecoaching.com

www.ingramcontent.com/pod-product-compliance
Lightning Source LLC
Chambersburg PA
CBHW041146050326
40689CB00001B/500